AN ARMENIAN FAMILY

AN ARMENIAN FAMILY

By Keith Elliot Greenberg

 Lerner Publications Company • Minneapolis

The interviews for this book were conducted in the fall of 1995 and in 1996.

This book is available in two editions:
Library binding by Lerner Publications Company
Soft cover by First Avenue Editions
241 First Avenue North
Minneapolis, MN 55401
ISBN: 0-8225-3409-6 (lib. bdg.)
ISBN: 0-8225-9775-6 (pbk.)

A pronunciation guide can be found on page 54.

LIBRARY OF CONGRESS CATALOGING-IN-PUBLICATION DATA

Greenberg, Keith Elliot.
    An Armenian family / Keith Elliot Greenberg.
        p.   cm. — (Journey between two worlds)
    Includes bibliographical references and index.
    Summary: Chronicles the history of the Armenian people and describes the experiences of one Armenian family who left Russia to rebuild their lives in America.
    ISBN 0-8225-3409-6 (lib. bdg. : alk. paper)
    1. Armenian American families—New York (State)—New York—Juvenile literature. 2. Armenian Americans—New York (State)—New York—Juvenile literature. 3. Brooklyn (New York, N.Y.)—Social life and custome—Juvenile literature. 4. New York (N.Y.)—Social life and customs—Juvenile literature. 5. Refugees—New York (State)—New York—Juvenile literature. 6. Armenians—Azerbaijan—Nagorno-Karabakh—Juvenile literature. 7. Nagorno-Karabakh (Ajerbaijan)—Emigration and immigration—Juvenile literature. [1. Armenian Americans. 2. Refugees. 3. Armenians—History.] I. Title. II. Series.
    F129.B7G69   1997
    974.7'100491992—dc20   96-17184

Manufactured in the United States of America
1 2 3 4 5 6 - JR - 02 01 00 99 98 97

AUTHOR'S NOTE

The author wishes to thank each member of the Asriyan and the Melik-Mirzakhan families for their hospitality, cooperation, and intriguing stories. Additionally, he would like to thank Christopher Zakian and Michael Guglielmo of the Diocese of the Armenian Church of America in New York for their assistance on this project. Special thanks to Aram Arkun at the Diocese of the Armenian Church of America in New York for his translation from Armenian into English of the poem on page 23.

FAMILY'S NOTE

Our mother and grandmother, Viktoriya Mirzoyan, worked as a physician in Baku for 40 years. We wish to thank her Jewish, Azeri, and Russian patients and friends who helped our family escape from Baku. We express thanks to Albert's sister Ruzanna and her husband, Vladimir Akopdzhanov, living in the United States. They contacted the Lutheran Church, which then served as our sponsor. We are indebted to Albert's friend and colleague, the composer Boris Vishnevkin, our spiritual sponsor. Boris and his family helped us to navigate our new lives in the United States. And we thank God.

SERIES INTRODUCTION

U What they have left behind is sometimes a living nightmare of war and hunger that most Americans can hardly begin to imagine. As refugees set out to start a new life in another country, they are torn by many feelings. They may wish they didn't have to leave their homeland. They may fear giving up the only life they have ever known. Many may also feel excitement and hope as they struggle to build a better life in a new country.

People who move from one place to another are called migrants. Two types of migrants are immigrants and refugees. Immigrants choose to leave their homelands, usually to improve their standards of living. They may be leaving behind poverty, famine (hunger), or a failing economy. They may be pursuing a better job or reuniting with family members.

Refugees, on the other hand, often have no choice but to flee their homeland to protect their own personal safety. How could anyone be in so much danger?

Vendors sell flowers at a farmers market (above) *in Baku, the capital of Azerbaijan.* (Facing page) *A couple mourns the loss of a family member, who is buried in a military cemetery in Nagorno-Karabakh, a region in Azerbaijan. The region has been a center of conflict since 1988, when Armenia and Azerbaijan—then both Soviet republics—began fighting over control of the area.*

The conflict that began in Nagorno-Karabakh quickly spread to other parts of Azerbaijan and to neighboring Armenia. A bread merchant (above) sets up shop in a makeshift marketplace in Yerevan, the capital of Armenia.

The government of his or her country is either unable or unwilling to protect its citizens from persecution, or cruel treatment. In many cases, the government is actually the cause of the persecution. Government leaders or another group within the country may be persecuting anyone of a certain race, religion, or ethnic background. Or they may persecute those who belong to a particular social group or who hold political opinions that are not accepted by the government.

From the 1950s through the mid-1970s, the number of refugees worldwide held steady at between 1.5 and 2.5 million. The number began to rise sharply in 1976. By the mid-1990s, it approached 20 million. These figures do not include people who are fleeing disasters such as famine (estimated to be at least 10 million). Nor do they include those who are forced to leave their homes but stay within their own countries (about 27 million).

As this rise in refugees and other migrants continues, countries that have long welcomed newcomers are beginning to close their doors. Some U.S. citizens question whether the United States should accept refugees when it cannot even meet the needs of all its own people. On the other hand, experts point out that the number of refugees is small—less than 20 percent of all migrants worldwide—so refugees really don't have a very big impact on the nation. Still others suggest that the tide of refugees could be slowed through greater efforts to address the problems that force people to flee. There are no easy answers in this ongoing debate.

This book is one in a series called *Journey Between Two Worlds*, which looks at the lives of refugee families—their difficulties and triumphs. Each book describes the journey of a family from their homeland to the United States and how they adjust to a new life in America while still preserving traditions from their homeland. The series makes no attempt to join the debate about refugees. Instead, *Journey Between Two Worlds* hopes to give readers a better understanding of the daily struggles and joys of a refugee family.

Soldiers in Nagorno-Karabakh keep a lookout for enemy soldiers.

On a Friday night, Julie-Anna Asriyan and her family gather in her living room in Brooklyn, New York. Julie-Anna's parents are there, along with her little sister, her aunt, her grandfather, and her cousins. The television goes off, musical instruments come out of cases, and the Asriyans sing and play music. Sometimes the melodies are from Broadway shows—cheerful songs that make the family feel happy. But other songs remind them of the world they have left behind.

The Asriyans are Armenians, an ethnic group that has been chased, beaten, and killed in the many places they've lived. When Julie-Anna's mother, Ivetta, sings the Armenian song "Karavan," the mood in the room turns sad.

Julie-Anna's family (clockwise from center, *Kristina, Alexander, Julie-Anna, Alexander, Viktoriya, Ida, Ivetta, and Albert*) *gather for an evening of lively entertainment.*

"Karavan" is a song about being a refugee, forced from your home, forced to run to another place. You hope you'll be safe there, but usually you aren't. Once again you find yourself in danger, and you have to keep running. Sometimes the people in the song think they hear their neighbors calling them back. But it is only a dream. Forever and ever the refugees are fleeing, using the ground instead of a mattress, a rock instead of a pillow, searching for a place to call home.

The song tells the story of the Armenian people. It also tells the story of Julie-Anna's family.

Julie-Anna (facing page, left) *enjoys painting with watercolors. She tackles many subjects in her artwork, including soldiers and flowers* (above).

 Julie-Anna is 12 years old. She lives in the second-floor apartment of a two-family house in Sea Gate, a quiet community in Brooklyn, the most populated borough (section) of New York City. Sea Gate is on Coney Island—home of New York's famous amusement area and the Cyclone, a popular roller-coaster ride. A seventh grader, Julie-Anna plays flute in her school's band. When she's alone, she paints with watercolors. One day she hopes to be an actress.

Julie-Anna and her 12-year-old cousin Alexander are in the same class. They ride the bus together to their school, about five miles (eight kilometers) away. To their classmates, Julie-Anna and Alexander seem no

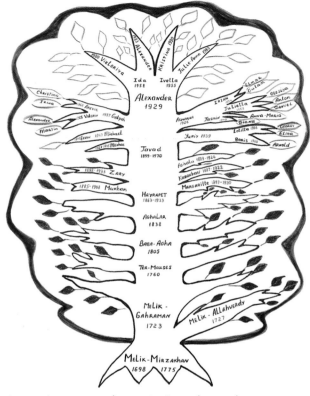

Ivetta's watercolor painting shows her family tree.

different than anyone else. Few people realize how much the two suffered in their old home, the former Soviet republic of Azerbaijan, just because they were Armenian.

"I never felt at home before I came here," Julie-Anna says. "Every time we moved somewhere, the people chased us out. Nobody wanted us until we came to Brooklyn. I didn't belong anywhere."

Armenia is located in a mountainous section of southwestern Asia. Over the centuries, the country was repeatedly conquered and divided. In ancient times, Persia (Iran) and Greece ruled Armenia. In about 100 B.C., a sizable Armenian empire extended into parts of what are now Iran, Syria, Lebanon, Turkey, and Azerbaijan. The expanding Roman Empire soon conquered Armenia but permitted it to operate somewhat independently.

Armenians practiced a religion that combined the faiths of the people of Persia and Greece with local pagan beliefs. But in the A.D. 300s, Armenia's king Tiridates III converted to Christianity. The rest of the country soon followed, and Armenia became the first official Christian nation in history.

Armenia's written language originated in A.D. 404, when a Christian monk named Mesrob created an Armenian alphabet. Afterward the Christian nation produced illustrated versions of the Bible (above) *with text in the Armenian language.*

After the death of Tiridates III in 330, part of Armenia fell into the hands of the Persian Empire. The Persians practiced the Zoroastrian religion. This faith preaches that there are two spirits–one of light and good, another of evil and darkness. The Armenians' Christian beliefs disturbed the Persians, who demanded that all Armenians accept Zoroastrianism.

Eventually Armenians rebelled against the order to convert. Led by Prince Vardan Mamikonian, they steadily fought Persian forces for more than 20 years. Even when the Armenians lost a battle, the Persians were impressed with their enemies' determination. In A.D. 451, after Prince Mamikonian was killed in a bloody battle, the Persians agreed to let Armenians practice Christianity. Armenians everywhere proudly remember this part of their history by celebrating Saint Vardan's Day every February.

In the early 600s, Arab peoples from the Middle East adopted a new religion called Islam. Soon afterward the Arabs conquered Persia, including Armenia, and tried to force the people to become Muslims, or followers of Islam. Religion became a major source of conflict between Christian Armenians and their Muslim rulers until 885, when the Arabs recognized Ashot I as the Christian king of Armenia.

Peace, however, was short-lived. The Turks conquered most of Armenia in 1071. Beginning in the

1200s, the Mongols, fierce warriors from central Asia, repeatedly attacked Armenia, causing much damage and bloodshed. By the 1600s, Armenia was again divided. The Turkish-ruled Ottoman Empire controlled western Armenia, and the Persians took over eastern Armenia. The Ottomans then went to war against the Persians, using Armenia as a battlefield. When either side retreated, its soldiers burned Armenian homes and farms. The defeated group felt it was better for the land to be destroyed than to fall into the hands of the enemy.

In the A.D. 400s, Prince Mamikonian (left) led the struggle against the Persians, who tried to force their religion on the Christian Armenians. About a thousand years later, the Ottoman Turks (above)—who followed the religion of Islam—conquered Armenia.

During the Armenian Genocide, which began in 1915, the Ottoman government deported hundreds of thousands of Armenians to the Syrian Desert, which lies in Syria to the south of modern-day Turkey. These Armenians are fleeing the deportation.

In 1828 and 1829, Russia occupied Persian Armenia. Under Russian leadership, Armenians were prohibited from speaking their language and building their own schools and churches. In western Armenia, which was still ruled by the Ottoman Empire, Armenians were commanded to convert to Islam and to adopt the Turkish culture. Many refused. In response the Turks massacred 200,000 Armenians between 1894 and 1896.

World War I (1914–1918) pitted the Ottoman Empire against many countries, including Russia. Armenia was caught in the middle. Fearing that the Armenians would side with the Russians, the Ottoman rulers took drastic action. They set off the worst event in Armenian history in 1915, when they killed 1.5 million people in what is known as the Armenian Genocide. Two-thirds of the Armenian citizens living in Ottoman-ruled territory were wiped out. Calling the Armenians traitors, Turkish troops led people from their homes and marched them deep into the Syrian Desert, where they were shot to death.

The Armenians who escaped the slaughter scattered all over the world, moving to Russia, Lebanon, France, Argentina, and the United States. In these and other places, Armenians did their best to keep their culture alive. By the 1990s, one million Armenians were living in North America. Boston, Philadelphia, Detroit, and Los Angeles all have large Armenian populations. Julie-Anna is one of 50,000 Armenians living in the New York City area.

Julie-Anna's ancestors are from Nagorno-Karabakh, a region of southwestern Asia isolated from Armenia by the Caucasus Mountains. The territory is about the size of Delaware. Most of the residents are Armenians or Turks. A minority of the population are Azeri. Azeris come from Azerbaijan, a republic where the main religion is Islam.

Many years ago, Nagorno-Karabakh was officially part of Armenia. In 1920 the Soviet Union took over

Muslims, who practice the faith of Islam, pray inside a mosque (Islamic place of worship) in Azerbaijan.

northwestern Armenia. Soviet authorities were worried about how to control Transcaucasia—a rugged region that includes all of Armenia, Azerbaijan, and Georgia. The Soviets considered the people who lived in this area to be stubborn and independent. Soviet leaders feared that these groups would not always obey orders. The best way to govern Transcaucasia, the authorities reasoned, was by pitting the different peoples against each other.

In 1922 a Soviet official named Joseph Stalin—who would later become dictator of the Soviet Union—ordered that Nagorno-Karabakh be given to neighboring Azerbaijan, the land of the Azeri people. Stalin believed that it would be easier to control the Armenians of Nagorno-Karabakh if they were cut off from Armenia. Ever since then, Armenians and Azeris have disagreed about who should own the land.

The Caucusus Mountains stretch between the Black Sea in the northwest and the Caspian Sea in the southeast. The rugged range is rich in mineral resources such as oil, coal, and copper. Farmers raise crops and herd livestock on the hilly slopes.

 Julie-Anna's mother, Ivetta, can trace her family's history in Nagorno-Karabakh back to the year 1514. The family is descended from a khan, or ruler, of a section of the territory called Askeran. Ivetta's maiden name, Mirzoyan, is a shortened version of Melik-Mirzakhan. In Armenian the word *melik* means "king." The *khan* in Mirzakhan

A woman (right) strolls through the old part of the city of Baku, Azerbaijan. Nagorno-Karabakh became a part of Azerbaijan in the 1920s, under the orders of Joseph Stalin (below).

means "leader." After the Soviets took over Armenia and Nagorno-Karabakh, they tried to erase the memory of powerful Armenian leaders from the past. Both "melik" and "khan" were eliminated from the family name, which became Mirzoyan.

Alexander—Ivetta's father and Julie-Anna's grandfather—was born in 1929. At one time, his family owned a great deal of land, on which they raised fruits, vegetables, and livestock. But the family's property was gradually seized by the Soviet government. As Alexander grew up, he found it difficult to make a living near his home. In 1949 he left Nagorno-Karabakh for Baku, the capital of Azerbaijan, located on the Caspian Sea. There he enrolled at the Oil and Chemistry Industrial University, where he studied engineering.

21

It hurt Alexander to leave his hometown. It also pained him to see the restrictions the Soviet Union placed on the Armenian language. Children's books and, later, radio and television, were required to be in Russian, the official language of the Soviet Union.

In Baku Alexander became an engineer. In 1953 he married Viktoriya, an Armenian doctor at the local hospital. Viktoriya was a very talented woman. She played the mandolin and spoke six languages: Armenian, Russian, Georgian, German, Turkish, and Yiddish—a tongue spoken by Jewish people in the area.

Alexander never forgot his love of Armenian. He wrote poems in the language—poems he recites in the family's home in Brooklyn. One poem talks about the agony of leaving Nagorno-Karabakh—the same sorrow a person might feel about leaving a mother. At night, the poem continues, the writer sees the land again in his sleep.

Alexander and Viktoriya had two children, Ivetta and Ida, both born in Baku. While growing up, the sisters were very close to a male cousin named Karen. Karen's father died while his wife was pregnant with the boy. Later, Karen and his mother, Amaliya, moved into Alexander's house. Ivetta's father looked after Karen and raised him like a son. Ivetta always considered Karen to be her brother. When Julie-Anna was a little girl, she thought of Karen as her uncle.

Julie-Anna's Grandfather Alexander met his wife Viktoriya (above) *in Baku, where she was a well-known doctor.*

KHNDZORESTAN

The following poem is by Alexander Mirzoyan, Julie-Anna's grandfather (pictured as a young man above). Translated from Armenian, the poem is dedicated to the poet's mother village in Nagorno-Karabakh.

My village, my beloved
My village, progenitor of all,
In the bosom of Artsakh
Mourning with my nation.

You, my fountain of milk
Allow me to give you a kiss.
Let me satisfy my longing,
Let me give the anguish of my soul.

My village, my cradle
My village, childhood home.
I am always with you
Asleep or awake.

Where are you now? Where,
My Lachin fountain
My forest pasture?
I miss you.

My village, unparalleled
My village, my abode.
I am dying for your view,
Your home and portal.

Distant, I am too distant
From you to die.
My living soul
I will send to you.

Behold, it is thus. I wish that I turn to dust.
Let me lie under my nation's feet,
not another's.

Armenians have a long history as Christians. The church (left) *near Echmiadzin, Armenia, was built in* A.D. *618. The altar* (below) *inside the church features a painting of Mary and Jesus, central figures in the Christian religion.*

 Soviet rule was often unfair, but the Mirzoyan family experienced much success in the city of Baku. Ivetta became an opera singer and a grade-school teacher. Her sister, Ida, was also a teacher, an actress, and a singer.

In 1980 Ivetta married Albert Asriyan, a violinist and composer. Albert wrote songs for television shows. People all over the Soviet Union heard his music. But because Albert had an Armenian-sounding last name, it was sometimes left out of the television credits.

Julie-Anna—Ivetta and Albert's first child—was born in 1983. The three of them lived with Ivetta's family, so Julie-Anna spent a lot of time with her maternal grandparents, her Aunt Ida, and Ida's children—Alexander and Viktoriya. Viktoriya is two years older than Julie-Anna. The three children played together and with neighborhood kids of many backgrounds, including Armenians, Azeris, Jews, and Russians.

Baku had two Armenian churches. The larger one was shaped like a typical Armenian cathedral. From a bird's-eye view, the building looked like a cross. But the Soviet government sometimes made life difficult for people who openly practiced their religion. The government, for instance, did not allow church members to attend college or to get a good job. Because of this, many Armenians did not baptize their children. Instead of celebrating Christmas, presents were exchanged on New Year's, a day with no religious meaning. Still, the Asriyans did participate in some Easter traditions. They'd make Armenian-style Easter eggs—white on top, with sparkles on the sides—and share them with their Azeri friends.

"Everything seemed okay," says Ida. "Of course we knew that many people didn't like Armenians, didn't want Armenians living next to them. But we had good jobs, so we pretended that nothing was wrong."

Because Viktoriya was a well-liked doctor, she didn't think the family would ever face any danger. Many of Viktoriya's closest friends were Azeris. And she'd delivered hundreds of babies of various ethnic backgrounds. She never imagined that some of these children would grow up to attack the family.

In Baku Ida was an actress, a singer, and a teacher of history and philosophy.

The trouble for Julie-Anna's family began not in their home city of Baku but in Nagorno-Karabakh—the place where Alexander, Julie-Anna's grandfather, was born. In 1985 Mikhail Gorbachev became the leader of the Soviet Union. He eased some of the Soviet Union's strict laws, an approach he called glasnost. The policy permitted people to do and say things that other Soviet leaders had not allowed. Finally, individuals could go to church, could criticize the government, and could read whatever they wished—without fear of punishment. Unfortunately, this new freedom also enabled groups that had been silent enemies to renew their battles. In both Armenia and Azerbaijan, Christians and Muslims were soon locked in violent conflict.

A woman and her daughter walk along a street in Stepanakert, the main urban center in Nagorno-Karabakh. Fighting between Armenians and Azeris has badly damaged the city.

In Nagorno-Karabakh, Armenians declared that they wanted the region to be independent. In February 1988, one million Armenians marched through their capital, Yerevan, demanding change. The next day, busloads of Azeris broke windows of Armenian homes and attacked Christians in the city of Sumgait, about 15 miles (24 km) northeast of Baku in Azerbaijan. The bloodshed soon spread to Baku, where Julie-Anna lived. Hundreds of people died, and thousands were injured. About 150,000 Christians escaped to Armenia.

Residents of Yerevan, Armenia, can see Mount Ararat from their city. The peak rises in nearby Turkey.

Meanwhile, in Nagorno-Karabakh and in Armenia, Azeris found themselves being attacked by groups of Armenians. On both sides, most people simply wanted to live in peace. But some people felt that the only way to gain control of Nagorno-Karabakh was to fight for it. Over the following five years, the violence became so severe that one million Armenians and Azeris became refugees.

Julie-Anna was five when Baku exploded in riots. She remembers looking out her window and seeing smoke drifting up to the sky. Gangs were setting Armenian-owned property on fire.

Despite the danger, Julie-Anna's family didn't want to leave Baku. Julie-Anna's parents were born there, and they didn't know any other home. About one-third of the city's population was Armenian. They couldn't *all* be forced out. The family prayed that the bad times would pass. But the situation only got worse.

Mobs of Muslim Azeris were stopping city buses and entering the vehicles. "Who's Armenian here?" the intruders would ask. Anyone who admitted to being Christian was kicked off.

In the early 1990s, Azeris, Russians, and Armenians were the largest ethnic groups in Azerbaijan. But since then, many Russians and Armenians have fled the nation to escape ethnic violence.

Armenian fighters in Nagorno-Karabakh take cover in a trench.

In the elevator in Ida's apartment building, somebody painted the slogan, "No Armenians Allowed!"

Some Armenians tucked their necklaces—with Christian crosses—underneath their clothes so other people wouldn't recognize them as Christians. A few Armenian families changed their names to Azeri-sounding ones. Most Armenians had an *an* at the end of their last names, while Azeris had an *ev*. Had the Asriyans wanted to appear Azeri, for example, they would have switched their name to Asriyev.

Local authorities turned off the heat in Armenian homes in the middle of winter. Julie-Anna's family would receive phone calls late at night. "You're lucky you're still alive," the callers said. "Get out of Azerbaijan before it's too late."

Students at Viktoriya's school would threaten her. "What are you Armenians still doing here?" they said. "You better move fast and go back to Armenia."

Once, a furious crowd surrounded Ida while she rode the bus. "Are you Armenian?" they asked.

Ida had to think quickly. The mob wanted to throw her off the vehicle as it moved through Baku's streets. "No," the actress lied. "I'm Jewish." In Baku the battle was between Muslims and Christians. Jews weren't involved. The pack believed Ida, and they let her go.

Another time a large group stormed into the theater where Ida was performing. "Which of the actors are Armenian?" they shouted. A few men stepped forward and were immediately beaten. But several of the Azeri actors were disgusted by what they saw. They quietly snuck Ida and other Armenians out of the building, while the gang's attention was elsewhere.

A troupe presents a traditional Armenian folk dance. While acting in a play at a theater in Baku, Ida was threatened by a gang who came to harass Armenians.

The domes of Saint Basil's Cathedral rise in the center of Moscow, the capital of Russia. Ivetta traveled to Moscow in 1989 to get permission from the U.S. Embassy for her family to resettle in the United States.

This wasn't the only time Julie-Anna's family was helped by their Muslim friends. One day her grandfather Michael (Albert's father) was attacked in the street. Suddenly a group of his Azeri neighbors ran over to the crowd.

"Leave him alone," one man said.

"Why are you defending him?" a member of the mob yelled. "He's Armenian."

"No, he's not," the man lied. "He's Azeri—I've known him for years. There are no Armenians around here. Go home."

The crowd believed the story. They left and Julie-Anna's grandfather's life was saved. But not everyone was so lucky. When the grandfather of one of Viktoriya's friends was surrounded one day, he tried to fight off his attackers with an ax. The gang took the ax from the elderly man and killed him.

Every day, it seemed, Julie-Anna and her family heard stories like this. People didn't talk much about work, school, or holidays. They exchanged reports about which Armenians had been beaten or murdered.

In 1989 Ivetta traveled to the U.S. Embassy in Moscow, Russia. Azerbaijan was overwhelmed by violence, she told a representative of the U.S. government. As an Armenian, she believed she and her family would be safer in America. Ivetta filled out an application and returned to Baku to wait for a response.

An old family photo shows Viktoriya, Julie-Anna's grandmother, with one of her patients.

Julie-Anna's family began going to bed each night fully clothed. If their home was firebombed, or a gang burst in, they wanted to be able to run. Too many others in Baku had been attacked in the middle of the night and forced to flee Azerbaijan wearing only pajamas and slippers.

With each passing day, Armenians appeared to be in greater danger. Julie-Anna's grandfather Alexander went to work one day, only to see his watch-repair business set on fire. Letters arrived at the house, tormenting the family. "If you don't leave now, you will all die," the messages stated.

When Julie-Anna's cousin Alexander was in kindergarten, an incident occurred that terrified the Asriyans. The cook at school baked poison cookies. Then he asked the Armenian students if they were in the mood for a treat. Alexander ate a cookie and soon fell ill.

For days Alexander battled a raging fever. He vomited almost constantly. Many times the boy seemed to be on the verge of death. Fortunately his grandmother was a doctor. She tended Alexander around the clock, giving him medicine and slowly nursing him back to health.

One cold autumn day in 1989, while Baku was swept up in anti-Armenian demonstrations, Julie-Anna's grandparents gathered the family together. Grandmother Viktoriya said that many of her Azeri friends were worried about her safety. "We want you to go before you get hurt," they told her.

Julie-Anna's grandfather knew they were right. "We can't live here anymore," Alexander said. "A lot of the Azeris are nice people, but there are too many fanatics here, too many people who won't be happy until we leave or we're dead. We shouldn't wait around for them to kill us."

Karen and his wife and children had already left Azerbaijan—after his mother was beaten up, his car burned, and his daughter's life was threatened. They found a place to live in southern Russia. The Asriyans thought maybe they should go to Russia, too.

As the demonstrations outside grew louder, the family's fear increased. Afraid they would be attacked at any moment, they quickly fled. All they brought were clothes and photo albums—memories of times, both happy and sad, in Azerbaijan.

 The children and their grandfather Alexander soon joined Karen. Meanwhile Ivetta and Albert went to Moscow, Russia, to search for work and for housing for everybody. Ida remained in Baku, caring for her mother, the doctor, who was dying of cancer.

Tikhoretsk, the village in southern Russia where Julie-Anna traveled, was mainly inhabited by Cossacks, descendants of peasant warriors who'd served as horsemen in the Russian army many years before. Because the Cossacks had fought against the Communists before they gained control of Russia in the early 1900s, the Soviets punished the Cossacks. Soviet leaders forced Cossack villagers to relocate to other parts of the country. When Julie-Anna's family arrived, they found a close-knit farming community, where residents were suspicious of outsiders.

"We never felt like we were wanted there," Julie-Anna's cousin Viktoriya says. "We were city people

Armenian fighters aim their weapons at an Azeri town in Nagorno-Karabakh.

Julie-Anna, her cousins, and her grandfather joined Karen and his family in Tikhoretsk, Russia, where most of the residents were farmers (left).

and they were country people. We were Armenians and they were Cossacks. We knew we weren't going to stay there too long."

Ivetta was having a tough time finding work in Moscow. Many residents there were prejudiced against darker skinned people from throughout the Soviet Union—Chechen, Georgians, Azeris, and Armenians, among others. Although Julie-Anna's family appears white in the United States, in Moscow some people hatefully called Armenians "blacks." The best jobs were likely to go to people whose families originally came from Russia.

Julie-Anna's father, Albert, was lucky to find a job playing Jewish music at a theater and restaurant. He sent for the rest of the family, and they tried to start fresh in Moscow. They moved into a hotel filled with other Armenian refugees. While parents worked to support their families, the children living in the building played together and went to school.

The brightest moment for the family in Moscow came on Christmas Day in 1990, when Julie-Anna's sister, Kristina, was born. Because of glasnost, restrictions against religion had ended, and the family baptized the baby in an Armenian church in Moscow.

But overall, life in the Russian capital was difficult for the Asriyans. Many times, when Albert was walking home from work at night, the police would stop him in the street. "What are you doing around here, black man?" the officers would ask. Even after Albert explained that he worked at night, he'd often be taken to the police station and questioned further before being released.

In school some Russian children would taunt Julie-Anna and her cousins. "You don't belong here, blackie," they'd say.

Viktoriya tried to reason with them. "We're refugees," she said. "We were kicked out of our home in Azerbaijan. We have no place else to go."

"Well, don't come here," the kids replied. "Russia is for Russian people only."

The Soviet Union broke up in 1991. What had once been an orderly country now experienced a lot of crime and unemployment. Many families became desperate for food and jobs. Some Russians took out their frustration on Armenians and other non-Russians.

"You Armenians come here and take over everything," Julie-Anna's family was told. "You move into our buildings, so there's no room for Russians. You eat up all our food, so the rest of us are hungry."

After Julie-Anna and her family moved to Moscow, many of Julie-Anna's Russian classmates did not welcome her or her cousins.

Ivetta and Alexander hold up special passports from the Russian government that allowed the family to leave Russia for the United States.

In 1992 someone from the U.S. Embassy in Moscow responded to Ivetta's 1989 application to immigrate. Ivetta and her father, Alexander, were interviewed by a U.S. government official who tried to make sure the Asriyans knew what they were getting into.

"Everybody thinks America is so great," he said. "It's really not worth going there. All you hear about are all the good things. Well, there's a lot of bad there, too. Poor people are everywhere. And even Americans can't find jobs. What makes you think that you will?"

"God will help us," Alexander said.

The man pulled an American dollar bill from his pocket. "Don't talk about God," he scolded. *"This* is

The Statue of Liberty in New York welcomes immigrants to the United States.

god in America. And you will never make any money if you can't speak English."

Julie-Anna's grandfather persisted. "I am a refugee," he said. "I have spent my entire life running and running and running. First, I was in Nagorno-Karabakh. Then I had to go to Baku. Then we were chased here to Moscow. I'm an old man now. I can't run anymore. I know that America is a democratic country, and people will be fair to us. No one will chase me away."

Remarkably, Alexander's words swayed the man. He approved the application. Albert's sister Ruzanna had moved to New Jersey with her family in 1992. She agreed to sponsor, or help the family to adjust, when they arrived.

Julie-Anna, her parents, her grandfather, and her little sister were allowed to come to New York in 1993. Albert's parents, Michael and Cervart, also came to the United States that year. Unfortunately, Julie-Anna's grandmother Viktoriya died of cancer before having the chance to immigrate.

Ida had also applied to immigrate. She and her children, Alexander and Viktoriya, were permitted to join the other family members in 1994.

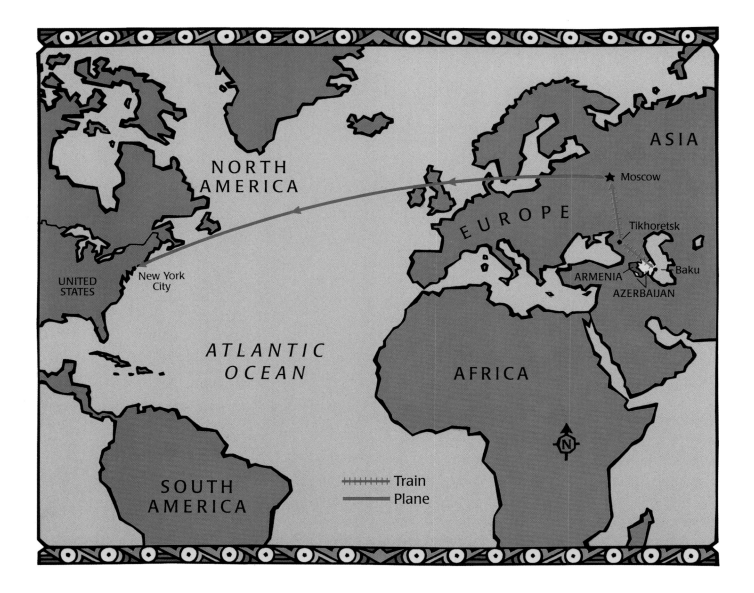

Alexander (center) *and his grandchildren* (left to right, *Kristina, Julie-Anna, Viktoriya, and Alexander*) *remember their journey to the United States. They hope Karen and his family will one day be able to come to New York.*

But cousin Karen—who grew up in the same home as Ivetta and Ida and was raised as a son by Alexander—could not get an application approved for his family. "We tried to explain that he was our brother," Ida says, with tears in her eyes. "He lived in our house. He was with us every day. But they said, 'No, he is not really your brother.' And he had to stay in Russia. Life is very hard for him and his family there. And every day we think of them. We won't be a whole family again until Karen and his family are living here in Brooklyn with us."

The family is trying to bring Karen to America. But because he's actually a cousin and not a brother, he has not qualified to join them. To enter the United States, refugees who are out of danger usually need to have an immediate family member, such as a sibling or a parent, act as a sponsor.

As bad as the situation was in Moscow, Julie-Anna misses some things about her old home. In Moscow she made a best friend named Natasha, a girl of Russian background. After school the two would jump rope and play tag. Sometimes they slept over at each other's houses. Although Julie-Anna has made friends in New York, she hasn't made one as special as Natasha.

Cousin Viktoriya also had friends in Moscow. When Viktoriya first arrived in New York, she missed playing with the other Armenian refugee children in the Moscow hotel. At times she felt bad and told her mother that she wanted to return to Moscow. But after Viktoriya made friends in Brooklyn, she decided that she liked America after all.

Julie-Anna greets a neighborhood dog in Brooklyn.

Julie-Anna (left), *Kristina* (right), *and their cousin Viktoriya* (background) *play with their dolls.*

Julie-Anna does homework in her room after school.

As she had in Baku, Julie-Anna has neighbors in Brooklyn of many different backgrounds, including Italians, African Americans, and Jews. About one mile (1.6 km) from her home is a neighborhood called Brighton Beach. New Yorkers have nicknamed the area Little Odessa because most of the residents are Russian-speaking Jews from the Ukrainian city of Odessa. Russian groceries, video stores, and restaurants line the sidewalks. It is more common to hear Russian spoken on the street than English. Because they moved so close to Little Odessa, Julie-Anna's family had an easy time finding their way around New York. If they were lost or confused, they could always ask for help in Russian.

The Asriyans have seen a number of familiar faces in New York. Albert works at a Russian restaurant, playing the organ on weekdays and the violin on weekends. One of the members of his band was part of the Jewish group Albert played with in Moscow. Sometimes when the family is walking through Little Odessa, they run into friends they knew in Azerbaijan. When the Asriyans eat at a Brighton Beach restaurant called Baku, which specializes in food from their native city, they sometimes see former neighbors from Baku.

Despite their troubles in Azerbaijan, the family still has Azeri friends. Not long ago, a group of Azeri

Julie-Anna's father, Albert, plays the violin with a band in New York.

actors the family knew in Baku toured the United States, putting on shows. When they passed through New York, they stayed at Julie-Anna's house.

Julie-Anna started the fifth grade in Brooklyn and was nervous about not being able to speak English. Fortunately, a number of children in the class had Russian-speaking parents and also spoke Russian. When Julie-Anna couldn't figure out a lesson, those pupils translated for her. Her teacher was also very understanding and paid special attention to her. Within a year, Julie-Anna didn't need help anymore. She could speak English as well as students born in the United States spoke it.

"It's not so hard," she says.

Learning a new language is tougher for adults. Albert and Ivetta rely on Julie-Anna to help them when they're trying to communicate in English. Julie-Anna translates during visits to the doctor, calls to the telephone or electric company, and shopping trips. Friends phoning the apartment hear Julie-Anna's English-language message on the answering machine.

At home Julie-Anna, Kristina, Alexander, and Viktoriya easily mix Russian and English, switching back and forth from one language to another while they play. "Whatever word comes to my head first, I use," Julie-Anna says.

Julie-Anna goes over an assignment with her English teacher after class.

Julie-Anna chats with her family during a meal at home. Alexander (far left) *is the only family member who is fluent in Armenian. Ivetta and Ida understand the language, but their children all grew up speaking Russian.*

When the family watches television, they press a closed caption button on their remote control. This choice—designed for deaf viewers—flashes the dialogue (spoken words) across the screen. The family keeps a special Russian/English translating computer near the television set. If they don't understand a word, they type it into the computer and learn its Russian equivalent.

Julie-Anna and her relatives find it funny that so many Americans refer to them as Russians. When the Asriyans were in Russia, they recall, people told them to leave because they were Armenians. "A lot of people here don't know what an Armenian is," Julie-Anna says. "To them, we are just Russians because that is the language we speak at home."

The Asriyans enjoy going to church. Frequently they attend a Greek Orthodox church because it is nearby and the service is similar to the one in the Armenian church. But on special occasions, they make the trip into Manhattan, the center of New York City, and visit the large Armenian cathedral there.

Armenian Americans go to the cathedral for many reasons. Recent immigrants can receive a lot of help at the church. Social workers there assist Armenian refugees with paperwork, employment, and housing. If a family needs furniture, workers ask around to see if any member of the church has an extra couch or dresser. English classes are held in the building, as well as courses that teach the Armenian language and faith.

"I was always proud to be Armenian," Julie-Anna says. "But in Russia, people would look at you like you were bad. Over here, I can be who I am. People in Brooklyn are warm," Julie-Anna continues. "They're nicer than people I've known anywhere else. They really welcome you."

For important religious occasions, Julie-Anna and her family attend services at the Armenian cathedral in Manhattan.

Julie-Anna adds another Easter egg to the pile she and her family have painted.

In Brooklyn the family is able to keep many of their traditions. On Easter they continue to paint eggs in the Armenian style. In Little Odessa, they buy Russian cheese, candies, and pastries. At home Ivetta makes an Armenian bread called *keta*. She also prepares a round, baked item called *turni hatz*—which is similar to pita bread—and *gengalav hatz*, or breaded greens.

Before she came to the United States, Julie-Anna had never eaten Chinese, Japanese, or Italian food. In Brooklyn she and her family regularly sample all three. But, despite all the exotic meals available in New York, Julie-Anna's favorite is french fries with macaroni.

When she has the time, Julie-Anna visits the Coney Island arcades and the nearby aquarium. In October the family goes wild for Halloween—a holiday they didn't discover until they moved to Brooklyn.

"We love Halloween," Julie-Anna says. "I couldn't believe this holiday, putting on masks and trick-or-treating. It's fun."

The family enjoys other elements of the United States just as much. Julie-Anna's Aunt Ida writes for a magazine for Russian-speaking residents of the United States. Cousin Alexander collects basketball cards. Kristina participated in a beauty contest for young girls. Whenever someone new enters her home, Kristina runs to get the sash she wore on stage. In big letters, it announces, MISS AMERICAN PRINCESS.

The Asriyans feel welcome in the United States.

2 Not all Americans like the sight of new immigrants moving into their neighborhood. Some children have teased Julie-Anna and Alexander about their foreign accents. At first they dressed too formally. Even a teacher asked cousin Viktoriya, "Why don't you wear jeans? You look like you're going to the theater." Sometimes the children were called nerds because they wore awkward-looking clothes from Russia, rather than trendy, American styles.

When Julie-Anna and Alexander first arrived in Brooklyn, a group of African American kids picked on the two newcomers. There were several fights. Then one day, the African American children noticed Julie-Anna and Alexander on the same school bus. "You also go to this school?" they asked.

After Julie-Anna and her cousin had a chance to talk to the other children, they all realized they shared certain interests. They were in the same grade and had to study the same subjects.

"Now, everything's okay," Julie-Anna says. "We help each other with homework. We're all friends."

Julie-Anna believes it is easier to make friends at school in the United States. In Russia, she remembers, all the students wore uniforms and the teachers were very strict. "Over here the teachers are more like your friends," she notes. "They make you feel comfortable. And when kids feel comfortable, they act friendly."

Kristina practices a traditional dance in an Armenian costume Ivetta made for her.

Julie-Anna likes to visit the sites of Manhattan (left) *and to relax at the beach* (below) *with her cousin Viktoriya and other family members.*

Julie-Anna remembers gym being as important as math, science, and language classes in her old country. "Training for sports was like the military," she says. "If you were good in one sport, it became your career. Here, gym is just playing."

Viktoriya also finds the U.S. school system refreshing. "In the Soviet Union, people were rewarded because their parents were important members of the Communist party, not because they were smart," Viktoriya claims. "Students would cheat because they didn't trust the system. You don't have to do that here. If you study hard, you will get ahead."

Julie-Anna (center), *Alexander* (left), *and Viktoriya* (right) *have fun on the boardwalk on Coney Island.*

In Julie-Anna's living room, the Friday night family concert is continuing. They perform the Beatles' song "Yesterday" then switch to the theme from the musical *Hello Dolly.* Afterward they play songs by the Armenian composer Aram Khachaturian.

Albert plays the organ, coaching his daughter as she accompanies him on the flute. Her cousin Alexander plays the clarinet. Ivetta sings and Ida plays the piano. Kristina dances around the living room. Grandfather Alexander bobs his head up and down, enjoying the sounds of his family—refugees who've finally found a place to call home.

"Being a refugee has made me understand that it's wrong to be prejudiced," Julie-Anna says. "Black, white—that's not what people should worry about. People should see what they have in common with everyone, not what they have different."

FURTHER READING

Armenia. Minneapolis: Lerner Publications Company, 1992.

Azerbaijan. Minneapolis: Lerner Publications Company, 1992.

Bider, Djemma. *A Drop of Honey.* New York: Simon & Schuster, 1989.

Engholm, Christopher. *The Armenian Earthquake.* San Diego: Lucent Books, 1989.

Hogrogian, Nonny. *The Contest.* New York: Greenwillow Books, 1976.

Kheridan, David. *Finding Home.* New York: Greenwillow Books, 1981.

PRONUNCIATION GUIDE

Armenia (ahr-MEE-nee-uh)
Asriyan (AHS-ree-yahn)
Azerbaijan (az-uhr-by-JAHN)
Azeris (ah-ZEHR-eez)
Baku (bah-KOO)
Caucasus (KAW-kuh-suhs)
Chechen (cheh-CHEHN)
Cossack (KAW-sak)
gengalav hatz (JIHNG-gah-lah HAHTZ)
Gorbachev, Mikhail (gawr-buh-CHAWF, mih-KYL)
Islam (ihs-LAHM)
Ivetta (EE-veh-tah)
keta (KAT-ah)
Khachaturian, Aram (kahch-ah-TUR-yuhn, ahr-AHM)
Mirzoyan (meer-ZOHY-yahn)
Moscow (MAHS-kau)
Nagorno-Karabakh (nuh-GAWR-noh-KAHR-uh-bahk)
Odessa (oh-DEH-suh)
Tiridates (tihr-uh-DAYT-eez)
turni hatz (TOHR-nee HAHTZ)
Yerevan (yehr-uh-VAHN)
Zoroastrianism (zohr-uh-WAS-tree-uh-nih-zuhm)

INDEX

Armenia: borders and location of, 15; ethnic violence in, 16–19, 26, 29; fight for control of Nagorno-Karabakh, 7, 19–20, 28, 29; history of, 15–19; map of, 14
Armenian Genocide, 18–19
Armenians, 10; history of, 15–19; violence and harassment toward, 29–33, 34–35, 36–37
Ashot I, 16
Askeran (Nagorno-Karabakh), 20
Azerbaijan: escape from, 40; ethnic groups in, 19, 25, 29; ethnic violence in, 26, 27, 28, 29–33, 34–35; map of, 14; schools in, 21
Azeris, 19, 20, 25, 28, 29

Baku (Azerbaijan), 7, 21, 22, 25, 28, 29, 31, 33, 34
Brooklyn (New York), 10, 12, 13; friends in, 42, 50, 51

Caucasus Mountains, 19, 20
Cossacks, 35–36
customs, beliefs, and traditions, 10, 12, 25, 31, 49, 51

demonstrations, 34–35

food, 44, 49

glasnost, 26, 36–37
Gorbachev, Mikhail, 26

language, 16, 22, 44, 45–46, 47; learning English, 45–46, 48
Little Odessa (New York), 44, 49

Mamikonian, Prince Vardan, 16, 17
maps, 14, 40
Moscow (Russia), 32, 35, 36, 37, 38, 41, 42
music, 10, 11, 12, 24, 36, 44, 45, 53

Nagorno-Karabakh, 7, 8, 9, 19–21, 23, 26, 27, 28, 29, 30, 35

Ottoman Empire, 17–19

Persian Empire, 16–17
poetry, 22, 23

refugees, 7–9, 12, 19, 29, 36, 53
religion: Christianity, 15, 16, 17, 24, 25, 30, 48; Islam, 16, 17, 18, 19; Zoroastrianism, 16, 17
Russia, 18, 34, 35–36

Soviet Union, 19–20, 21, 22, 24, 25, 26, 35, 36, 37
Stalin, Joseph, 20, 21

Tiridates III, 15–16
Transcaucasia, 20

United States, 8–9, 32, 38–39, 41; schools and education in, 12, 44, 45, 50–52
U.S. Embassy in Moscow, 32, 38

Yerevan (Armenia), 8, 28

ABOUT THE AUTHOR

Keith Elliot Greenberg is a freelance journalist, author, and television producer specializing in real-life stories. His television credits include scripts for *America's Most Wanted, Real Life,* and *In Search of Peace,* a documentary chronicling the history of the United States in the United Nations. Mr. Greenberg has written dozens of nonfiction children's books on topics ranging from entertainment to homelessness to international terrorism. Other Lerner titles by Keith Elliot Greenberg include *Zack's Story, Runaways,* and *Out of the Gang.* A native New Yorker, Mr. Greenberg resides in Brooklyn.

PHOTO ACKNOWLEDGMENTS

Cover photographs by © J. C. Tordai / Panos Pictures (left) and © Carol Halebian (right). All inside photos, including cut-ins of the Armenian alphabet, by © Carol Halebian except the following: © J. C. Tordai / Panos Pictures, pp. 6, 8, 9, 27; Armenian Library and Museum of America, p. 16 (left); Hairenek Publications, p. 17 (left); UPI / Corbis-Bettmann, p. 18; Cultural and Tourism Office of the Turkish Embassy, p. 17 (right); © George Steinmetz, p. 19; © Eugene G. Schulz, pp. 7, 20, 24 (both), 31; National Archives, photo no. 306–NT–171445C, p. 21 (bottom); © John Spaull / Panos Pictures, pp. 21 (top), 29; © David Orr / Panos Pictures, p. 28; © Martin Adler / Panos Pictures, pp. 30, 35; Sergej Schachowskoj, p. 32; © Dan Buettner, p. 36; Jeff Greenberg, p. 37; Statue of Liberty National Monument, p. 39; Albert Asriyan, p. 45; All artwork and maps by Laura Westlund.